To re-order go to:

nancemaven.com

If you enjoyed this planner please consider leaving a review on amazon as it greatly helps us self-published authors/publishers.

Thank you!